Interview Cracking In First Attempt

@Copyright registered, Department of Higher Education, Ministry of Education, Government of India

(Extra Included Body language, Voice Tone and Resume Preparation)

FAQs, Assignment, Practical Test approaches, live interactions and precaution safeguards tricks

For Fresher/Experience/Professionals/Competitive Private/Government Interview Clearance Tips

HRAC Council

@Registered, Ministry of Development Commission, Government of India

By,
DR. JITENDRA KUMAR

AUTHOR NOTE

ABOUT THE AUTHOR

Dr. Jitendra Kumar worked for a multinational company as a Developer, Senior Software Engineer, and Technical Manager. He worked as a Computer Science Lecturer at an afflicted college. He holds a Law degree, and he

https://sites.google.com/view/ hraccouncil

worked as a Legal Advisor in a Legal firm to support the activities of civil and criminal matter disputes to frame the legal drafting to execute the application by the legal team department. He worked as a Chief District Secretary in Human Rights and Social Justice Mission. He is a Member of the District Board of the Anti-Crime Control Council. He worked as a Social Worker and participated in various organizations like NGO's, educational institutions, the defence DRDO, and legal department, serving society by organizing and motivating people towards their success in life. He is a Microsoft Certified Technology Specialist from Microsoft Corporation, USA, and holds the Forensic Digital Examiner certification. He engaged for the work and support to the authorized forensic department for the evidence detection, cyber security analysis and examining the objects or substances. He got appreciation and awarded in Nationwide blog creator contest for providing unique ideas in health care from Manipal Hospital and got appreciation for iconic inspired personalities from Legal Authorities and got Buddha Nilayam Star award from Tata Group in CSR activities and participated and appreciated in Criminal Law Essay

Writing Competition by Law Centre for Research in Criminal Justice Sciences where Centre or Government dedicated towards carrying out research in the niche area of Criminal Law. He has received honorary doctorate award in the field of Law Empowerment. He received Bharat Gaurav Ratna award in recognition of exemplary contribution, unwavering dedication. He is an Author and wrote a book Interview Cracking in first attempt which is worldwide published. He travelled abroad to Dubai, Saudi Arabia, for the engagement of the project activities. He worked as a Income Tax Associate in CA office for tax liabilities, tax savings and any tax disputes for their clients. He is certified in the Artificial Intelligence (AL) and Machine Learning (ML) from Top ranked prestigious public university (Indian Institute of Technology) IIT Hyderabad and worked in various project to research and development activities like robotics, Human Scream Detection and Analysis for Controlling Crime Rate and Signature and Face Recognition etc. Any query related to suggestions/complaints, please send to hraccouncil @gmail.com

Dr. Jitendra Kumar

Lawyer, Criminologist, Researcher, Author, Director

Member of the District Board of the National Anti-Crime Control Board. Former District Chief Secretary, Human Rights and Social Justice Mission

Founder, Chairman of the Board of Directors

ACKNOWLEDGEMENT

My thanks to the publication for allowing me to perform my skills. This book helps the candidate use their skills and experience to grow their personality and achieve success in the field of the organization and society. I was dedicated to writing a book about the success of a candidate who struggles for jobs or wants to achieve his or her goal of becoming successful. My thanks to all my family, friends and colleagues for their feedback. Thanks to the reviewers for their feedback and suggestions to improve the content of the book. I thank you all for your support and guidelines towards the success of my book.

HOW TO READ THE BOOK

The book is to be read first with the definition of the subject and then analysed. It is better to research the subject yourself to understand the subject of the title and overcome the conclusion of the subject. The question can arise, like how, why, and what scenario to understand the depth of the subject title. After that, the candidate understands the flow of the subject with the help of the image, pictorial form, data flow, flow chart, etc. to understand analytical and logical skills to improve their skills on the particular subject of the title. The content index page number to use to identify the particular topic and read the description of the subject. The candidate can use Google and YouTube searches to make his or her understanding of the topics clear. The candidate should draw the diagram that is covered in this book to understand the definition of the subjects. If the candidate draws the diagram himself or herself, then the flow of understanding will be cleared for the candidate to succeed in the interview.

OBJECTIVE OF THE BOOK

This book is beneficial for students, professionals, employees, workers, and staff in the private and government sectors. This book has a feature on how to crack the interview for the government competitive examination or a private company for clearing the professional interview. It has a live conversation about the interaction between the interviewee and interviewer. This book enhances the skills of the candidate to get the interview clear in the first round of the interview if they have gone through the entire content of the book. This book provides tips and techniques to clear the interview. The candidate must follow the guidelines of the book to improve their communication skills in front of the interview panel. This book provides a clear data flow diagram that makes it easy to understand the interview process and crack the interview. It covers interview-related competitive examinations like SSC, railways, civil services, banks, airlines, etc. There are techniques and methods to be followed by the candidate during the interview. There has been mention of what they do and do not do during the interview process. There has been a focus on physical and mental strength to improve communication between the candidate and the interview panel. This book is highly recommended and demanded by all, whether students or professionals. This book provides test-yourself questions and answers that will improve the knowledge and skills of the candidates. This book provides precautionary and preparation guidelines for creating a resume. The fresher candidate is rejected, and the candidate gets frustrated because the fresher candidate is facing the challenge of clearing the interview. Even though the experienced candidate also faces the issue of clearing the interview, the interview is a complete process in terms of the person's skills and general behaviour. If the candidate is skilled but the behaviour of the candidate is not good, then the candidate will not be selected. If the candidate has good behaviour but does not have good skills, then the candidate is not fit for the job and will not be selected. Hence, the candidate should have both skilled talent and good behaviour, which the interviewer or company is looking for in the right candidate. This book enhances the skills of digital communication and self-evaluation. Free Interview kit includes- Soft copy of Fresher's resume, Experience resume, Cover letter, etc.

CONTENTS

MODULE 1: INTERVIEW INTRODUCTION AND BACKGROUND OVERVIEW

PART 1: INTRODUCTION OF INTERVIEW COMMUNICATION

SECTION 1: OVERVIEW ABOUT INTERVIEW

An interview is the process of having a conversation between two people. The others who asked the question are called the interviewers, and those who answered the question are called the interviewees. The communication between the interviewer and interviewee establishes the relationship between the candidate seeking jobs and the interviewer or employer hiring the candidate. The interviewer will test the knowledge and skills of the candidate to determine whether he meets the requirements of the organization. The interviewer will try to ask all types of questions, like skills, technology, social, academic, cultural, achievements, management, etc., to measure the candidate's capacity for experience.

SECTION 2: FLOW CHART OF THE INTERVIEW ROUND

The candidate can get the questions like on to check basic communication, Eligibility (qualification, skills, experience, achievement, sports, and prizes), Salary expectation, Notice period and fit for the role position.

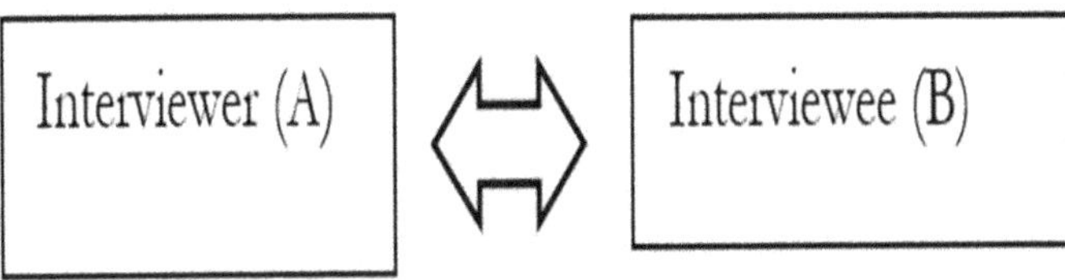

Figure: Interview round

SECTION 3: EXPLANATION OF THE FLOW CHART ON INTERVIEW

A is an interviewer, who is the person or organization (company, office, etc.) that has the authority to take the interview for the job seeker. A will evaluate the test conducted by the panel to select candidate B based on the performance of candidate. The requirements of the company should be matched to the particular skills of the candidate.

SECTION 4: OBJECTIVES OF THE INTERVIEW

The objectives of the interview-

1. To conduct the test to qualify the candidate
2. To verify the information from the candidature form
3. To know the necessary facts and information
4. To filter the ability of the candidate
5. To evaluate the candidature form
6. To measure the level of skills
7. To get to the analysis of additional information or skills of the candidate
8. To exchange ideas and views between two or more people.
9. To know the personal and professional information
10. To verify the already-submitted form or application of the candidate.
11. To know if the candidate is a fit for the requirements of the company
12. It is the complete process to identify the right candidate by the interviewer where candidate will initiate his or her ability to progress him-self or her-self towards the success in the interview.

PART 2: WHAT IS THE BACKGROUND AND HISTORY OF INTERVIEW?

SECTION 1: DESCRIPTION OF INTERVIEW HISTORY

The conduct of the Interview started around 1921. The interview was initiated to check the person's abilities and knowledge. The criteria of the interview are based on the skills of the person who attended the interview with a respected, skilled student or professional. During the incident time, the person was physically in the office to attend the interview, and mostly oral communication was exchanged at the premises or offices. Nowadays, digital communication makes it easier for candidates or job seekers to attend the interview. At the time of the incident, the candidate was walking into the office and submitting the resume to receive a call or invitation from the company. The company was also struggling to get a good candidate because, at the time, there was no social media or digital technology where the company could find a good candidate immediately.

SECTION 2: FLOWCHART OF THE INTERVIEW HISTORY

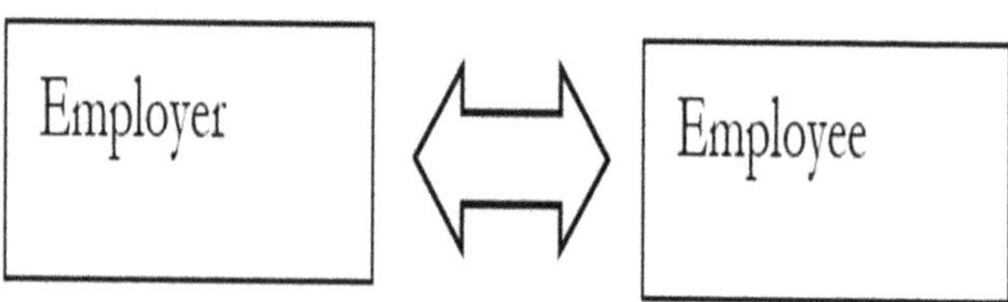

Figure: Interview channel

SECTION 3: EXPLANATION OF THE FLOW CHART ON HISTORY

An interview is the process of determining the ability and capability of a person who is skilled in a particular area or profession. The employer measures the efficiency, skills, and experience of the candidate and whether he or she fits the requirements of the company. The employer will ask questions of the Employee regarding his or her professional expertise in particular requirements of employment. Employees will answer questions asked by employers. The employee will answer in a very comfortable and polite manner. The job requirement is organized by the company or government authority to conduct interviews to get the right skilful candidate or employee.

PART 3: WHY INTERVIEW IS REQUIRED FOLLOW UP TECHNIQUES

SECTION 1: ABOUT NEEDED OF INTERVIEW KNOWLEDGE

Interview skills are an important part of any evaluation of knowledge and identify the depth of the particular skills or knowledge of the candidate. The interviewer will recognize you with the help of your expertise in the field of technology or any specific area. The interviewer will not focus on the other skills that do not match their requirements. Hence, the interviewer will be very clear to cross-verify the ability of the candidate's skills. So, the Interviewee who is attending the interview should have a clear understanding of their skills and abilities. If the Interviewee has no expertise in the specific areas, then it may be difficult for him or her to clear the interview.

SECTION 2: FLOWCHART OF THE INTERVIEW REQUIRED DETAILS

The candidate can get essential questions from the personal, professional, academic, technical, and behavioral information in during the interview.

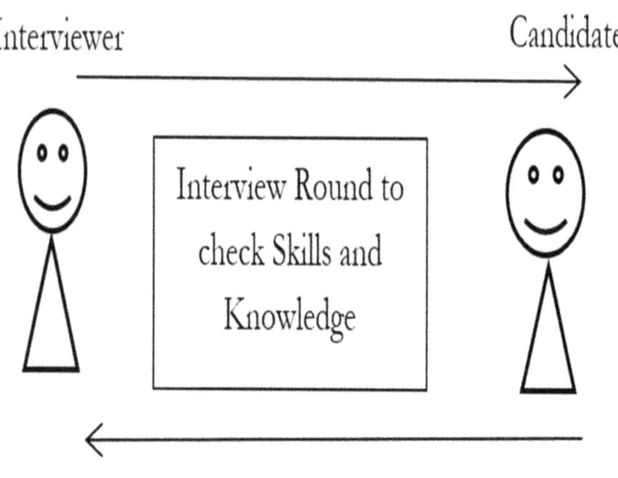

Figure: Interview needed

SECTION 3: EXPLANATION OF THE FLOW CHART ON INTERVIEW APPROACHES

The interviewer will observe the way of speaking of the candidate and how the candidate is delivering his or her speech and responding the answer in very precise way. The candidate must listen properly to the question asked by the interviewer to make sure the answer is correct for the relevant questions. The candidate can be rejected if the related answers do not match the required questions asked by the interviewer.

SECTION 4: TECHNICAL STEPS OF COMMUNICATION SKILLS

The candidate must explain their skills or knowledge in the following ways:

1. The speaking should be in precise and accurate explanation.
2. The knowledge should be relevant to the expertise areas.
3. The skills should be practised before attending the interview for the requirement applied.
4. The candidate must deliver the speech confidently.
5. The explanation should not be in fast or very slow speech.
6. Be calm and cool while explaining your skills or knowledge.
7. The topic or skills to be revised before attending the interview

MODULE 2: CAREER INTERVIEW SKILLS COMMUNICATION DIRECTION

PART 1: INTERVIEW SKILLS AND KNOWLEDGE DETERMINATION

SECTION 1: DESCRIPTION OF INTERVIEW SKILLS AND PERFECTION

The candidate's interview communication skills must be improved if they are to be successful on the interview panel. The most important part of the interview is for the candidate to communicate properly with the interviewer and explain the answer politely and descriptively to satisfy the interviewer. The interviewer will be focusing on the communication skills of the candidate to understand the behaviour of the candidate with technical or managerial skills.

SECTION 2: SELF-EVALUATION MEASURE TECHNIQUES

The following points of the candidate's self-evaluation are:

1. There should be practice of the skills and knowledge by the candidate himself or herself.
2. The way of writing is for the candidate to check the previous memory of the topics without seeing the topics or books to memorize the subjects.
3. Repeat twice or three times until the candidate remembers the topic covered for the technologies or skills.
4. The candidate will write on the paper and paste it on the wall to revisit the topic or skills.
5. Record your expertise and skills to remember them by listening to the audio or videos. Audio and video are more effective at capturing memories and making them memorable.

SECTION 3: FLOWCHART OF INTERVIEW KNOWLEDGE PROCESS

Below point makes the effective communications.

• Depth subject knowledge: The candidate should have must depth subject knowledge. The candidate answers with start with the concept give a real example and explain the impact area of the subject of the questions.

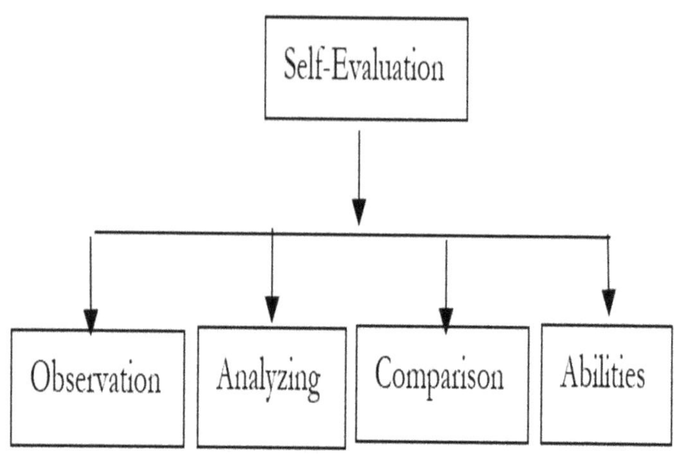

Figure: Interview self communication

SECTION 4: EXPLANATION OF FLOW CHART ON SKILLS PERFORMANCE

In the figure, we see that self-evaluation has four categories: observation, analysis, comparison, and abilities. Each category describes the self-evaluation measurement of the candidate for his or her abilities and talent in their expertise fields.

PART 2: SELF-EVALUATION TECHNIQUE

SECTION 1: ABOUT OF SELF EVALUATION

PROCESS TECHNIQUES

Carrier opportunity: we will talk about first what a carrier is, what a carrier makes, and how we can propose to get a better carrier opportunity. When the candidate prepares for the examination to get selected in any competitive examination for the private or government sector, he or she must clear the interview round first to get an offer or appointment letter from the organization. And about opportunity, which means that the candidate makes an effort to achieve something to get an opportunity in any field or respected area of the organization in his or her interest. Hence, carrier opportunity is a very important part of the candidate's success in the interview.

SECTION 2: FLOWCHART OF SELF-DETERMINATION SELECTION

Below point makes the effective communications.

• Ability to express: The candidate should express your own decision to explain the answers in during the interview. The communication of the exchanging the information should clear and concise manner in the interview by the candidate.

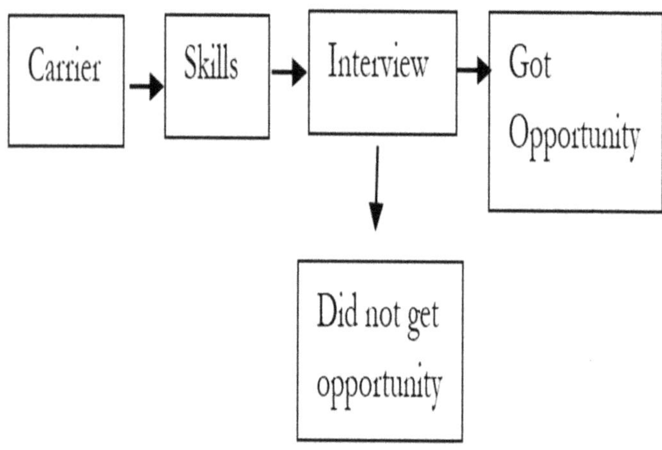

Figure: Interview opportunity

SECTION 3: EXPLANATION OF FLOW CHART ON SELF-STRONG TECHNIQUES

The self-strength technique is the process that starts with the carrier revolution of the candidate, and it goes to skills to verify that the candidate's expertise in the technology will get the right opportunity. If the candidate fails to satisfy the question asked by the interviewer, he or she may be rejected by the interviewer, and the candidate may not get the job in the current organization. If he or she can answer the question and satisfy the interviewer with his or her skills, then he or she may get the opportunity or offer.

PART 3: CAREER OPPORTUNITY EVALUATION PROCESS

SECTION 1: ABOUT CAREER CHALLENGES AND OPPORTUNITY

Before the interview, the candidate needs to prepare and revise the skills before attending the interview. The candidate should have planned for the success of the interview. He or she should note down the interview points, and accordingly, he or she should focus on the particular points to remember the topics. The candidate must check the existing questions that were asked by the interviewer previously to evaluate him or herself. So, then, the candidate can understand the previous questions and the patterns of the questions. The candidate should have the confidence to get cleared in the interview round. The candidate should have perfect body language while speaking in front of the interview panel.

SECTION 2: PRE-PLANNED INTERVIEW APPROACHES

Before the interview, the candidate must follow the below approaches:

1. Always have a happy and cool mind.
2. Do not be angry.
3. Think only positively.
4. Be on time at the premises.
5. Reach the venue in 10 to 15 minutes.
6. Keep your mobile in silent mode.
7. Wear your dress properly and clean it.
8. The dress should not be in any dark colour; make it a formal dress.
9. Shoes are preferred to formal black.
10. Preferable to saving your beard

SECTION 3: FLOWCHART OF CAREER GUIDELINES METHODOLOGIES

Below point makes the effective communications.

• Sell yourself: Like any product to explain to sell it with quality and benefits similarly to be introducing you in during the interview.

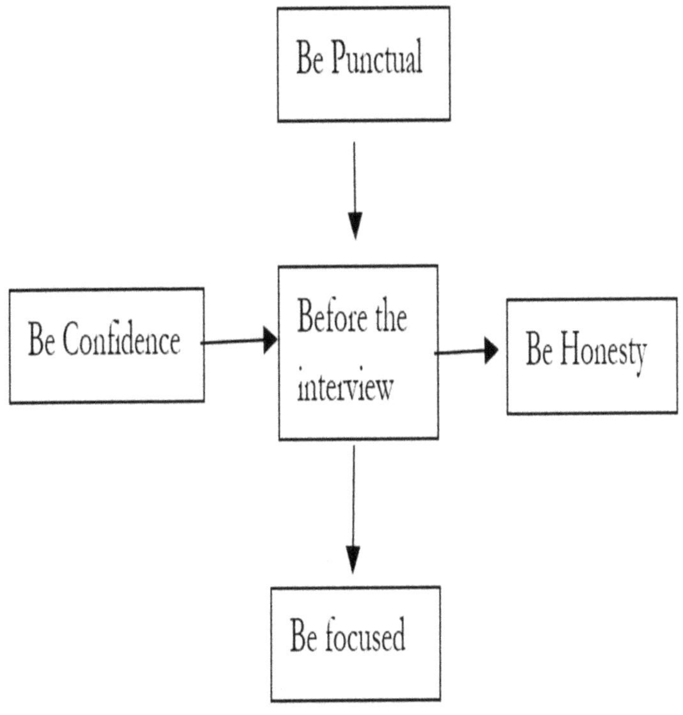

Figure: Inerview precaution

SECTION 4: EXPLANATION OF FLOW CHART ON CAREER PERSONALITIES

There are four main important categories, like confidence, focus, honesty, and punctuality, that a candidate should have ready before attending the interview. The first category is 'be confident, which means that the candidate will answer the question confidently. There should not be yes-and-no or confusion while speaking in front of the interviewer. The second category is 'be focused, meaning that the candidate will speak only about the question. There should not be manipulated answers given by the candidate that can be rejected by the interviewer immediately. The third category is 'honesty, which means that the candidate should speak the truth only. There should not be any assumptions about the answer to the questions. And the fourth category, being punctual, means that the candidate should be present at the venue location before the specified allocated time.

MODULE 3: INTERVIEW GUIDELINES AND RESEARCH METHODOLOGIES

PART 1: BEFORE THE INTERVIEW PROCESS AND GUIDELINES

SECTION 1: ABOUT BEFORE THE INTERVIEW TERMINOLOGY

The candidate should conduct research on the infrastructure and technologies of the organization to get true information about the organization. The employer or interviewer will be asking the question of whether they know our agencies or not. The job seeker must know the employment type and service that the company is offering to fit into the organization. If the candidate is looking for the job of engineer, but the company provides manufacturing and support activities that will not be relevant to the candidate, In the government sector, if you wish to apply for a doctor's job, you should be an MBBS holder, which will fit the requirements of the organization. Hence, the requirements of private or public agencies and candidate skills should match each other.

SECTION 2: FLOWCHART OF PRE-PLANNED INTERVIEW DIRECTION

The candidate should research on the organization, background, websites, services, products details, etc.

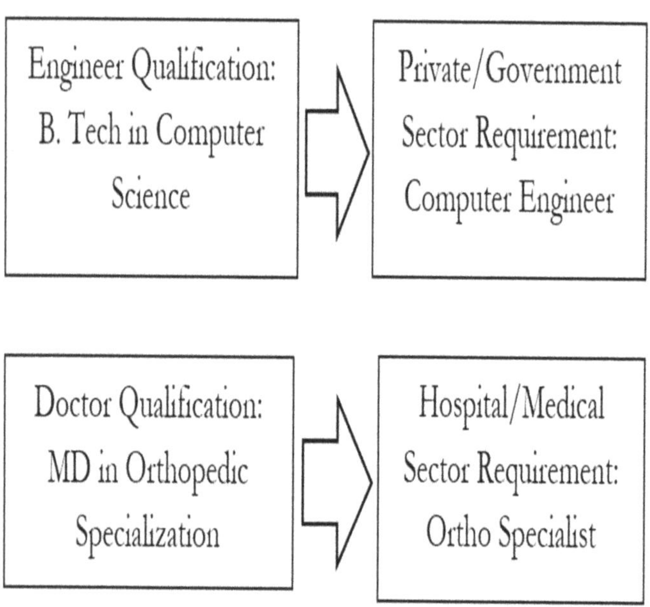

Figure: Interview direction

SECTION 3: EXPLANATION OF FLOW CHART ON PRE-PLANNED METHODOLOGIES

The specific skills of the candidates must fit the requirements of the organization. The candidate will be more concentrated and focused on the requirements of the organization, whether private or government agencies. The interviewer will offer those candidates who came for the same job type profile and performed better in the interview selection.

For example, doctors who have a specialization in orthopaedics are a fit-for-the-job type of specialist in a hospital. He will not fit in the support or insurance sectors. Similarly, engineers will not fit in the hospital to check the patient's diseases.

PART 2: RESEARCH METHODOLOGIES OF THE PRIVATE, GOVERNMENT JOB

SECTION 1: DESCRIBE OF RESEARCH METHODOLOGIES OF INTERVIEW

Practice makes perfect. The candidate will get the opportunity only by practicing the skills before attending the interview. When the interviewer asks the question in a practical way, it might be that the candidate is not able to answer it. If the candidate does not do research on the skills and does not practice interview skills, then there is less chance of getting an offer letter from the employer. The interviewer expects a deep and driven answer to understand the capability of the candidate and evaluate it against the requirements of the organization.

SECTION 2: FLOWCHART OF RESEARCH METHODOLOGIES TECHNIQUES

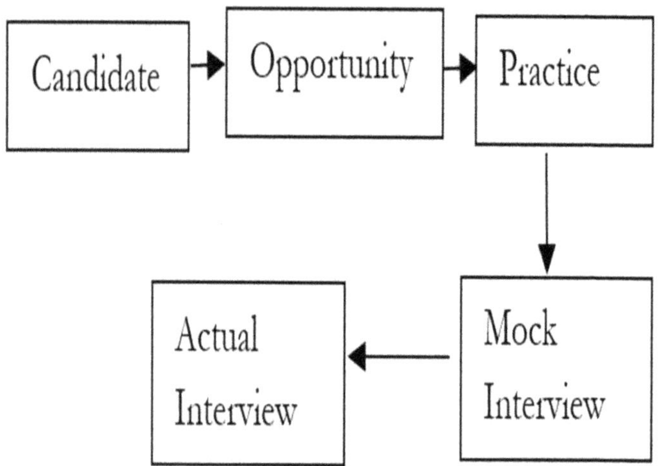

Figure: Interview research

SECTION 3: EXPLANATION OF FLOW CHART ON EMPLOYMENT PROCESS

The candidate will get the opportunity to stay at the venue and have time to revise their skills and knowledge. Once the candidate has practiced the skill set, he or she will be eligible to practice a mock interview. What is a mock interview? The mock interview is a kind of demo of pre-interview practice. The candidate makes sure to search and investigate the existing questions already asked to practice the set of interview questions and the skills. Once the mock interview is done, the candidate can attend the actual interview confidently and complete the round of interview tests successfully.

PART 3: OPPORTUNITY OF THE PRACTICE INTERVIEWS

SECTION 1: ABOUT OF OPPORTUNITY OF THE PRACTICE INTERVIEWS

The candidate's dress is the first impression in the interview. The candidate should wear a formal dress with formal shoes. There should not be more ornaments and rings to wear on the hand and neck. The candidate looks awesome in a formal dress. There should not be any distractions during the interview. The shirt should be plain in any color. The shirt's color should not be dark. It is better to prefer the shirt colour white. The paint should be black, or a blue colour will be preferable. The face should be washed, and a clean appearance will be preferable to attract the interviewer. Avoid jeans, t-shirts, and casual shoes in an interview.

SECTION 2: FLOWCHART OF OPPORTUNITY OF THE PRACTICE COMMUNICATION

There are below point makes the effective communications via practice interview communication with strong verbal and non-verbal soft skills.

• Always check yourself practically: Practice yourself in front of the mirror or record your voice or video. Check your tones of the language and try to correct it with re visiting the recorded videos.

• Check any learning websites: Check the practical conversations of the interviewer and interviewee communication and try to adopt it.

• Re write your mistake: Observe your mistake during the interview or self-practicing and try to correct it.

• Discuss with your friends: Talk with your friends to any group discussion topic and try to get feedback or your way of talking correction with friends and observe and correct it

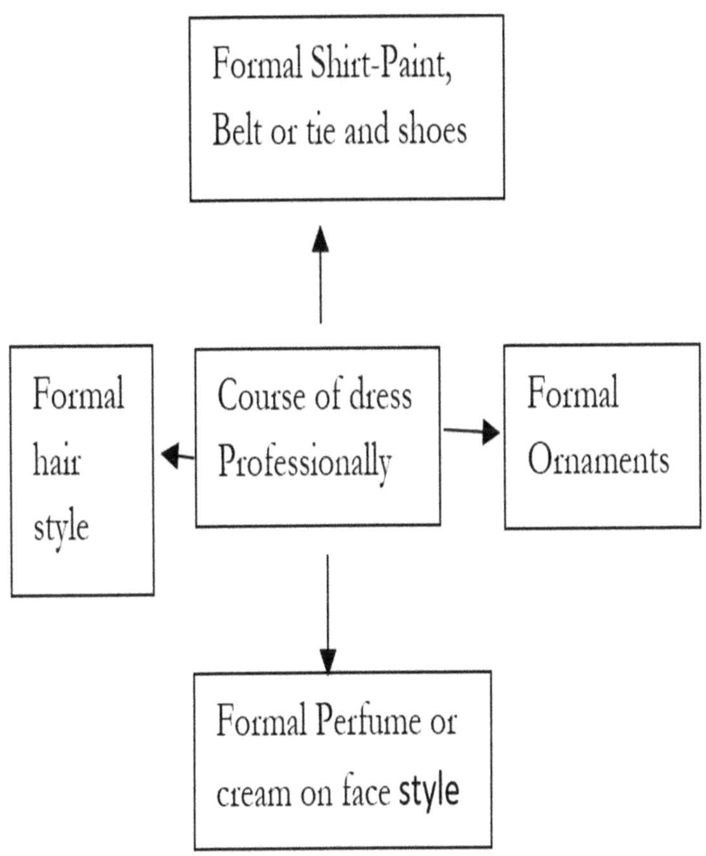

Figure: Interview practice

SECTION 3: EXPLANATION OF FLOW CHART ON OPPORTUNITY PROCESS

The candidate has four major categories: a formal shirt, paint, a belt or tie, and shoes. The second category is formal hairstyles. The third is formal ornamentation. The fourth is formal perfume or cream to use on the face or body. The first interviewer will look only at the candidate and observe his or her style of living, and then the interviewer will start communicating with the candidate.

MODULE 4: INTERVIEW RESPONSIBILITIES PROFESSIONALLY

PART 1: COURSE OF DRESS PROFESSIONALLY COMMUNICATION

SECTION 1: ABOUT COURSE OF DRESS OBJECTIVE

The candidate should arrive at the interview venue on time, 10 to 15 minutes earlier, to prepare their mindset to attend the interview. The arrival time should not exceed the time of the scheduled interview. If the candidate comes late, then the interviewer thinks that he or she is not interested in this job, which can lead to rejection in an interview based on a delay in reaching the interview location. Even though you are giving the answer correctly and answering very well, the interviewer will check not only the knowledge or skills of the candidate but also their intention, attitude, and punctuality towards the job profile.

SECTION 2: FLOWCHART OF COURSE OF DRESS DIRECTION

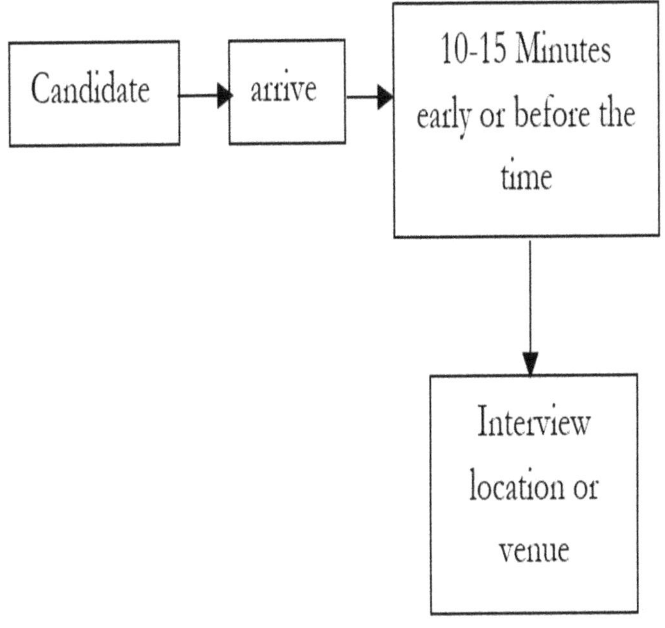

Figure: Interview course

SECTION 3: EXPLANATION OF FLOW CHART ON DRESS PERSONALITIES

The candidate has to follow the guidelines for attending the interview. The candidate will read the interview invitation or letter properly before attending the interview. The rules and regulations mentioned in the interview letter are to be accepted and followed up accordingly.

PART 2: RESPONSIBILITY OF ARRIVAL TIME

SECTION 1: DESCRIBE OF RESPONSIBILITY OF ARRIVAL TIME DISCIPLINE

The interview will start once the candidate enters the interview room. The candidate should enter the room very politely, with eyes contacting each other, and say good morning or Namaste. The interviewer will look at you at first glance to see how you enter the room and communicate with them. It's better to stand until someone says, please sit or have a seat. It impresses the interviewer as you wait for the interviewer to start politely and with discipline. Sit straight and in a cool, calm manner to listen to the questions from the interviewer. First, listen to the questions asked by the interviewer, then start speaking or explaining them properly without hesitation.

SECTION 2: FLOWCHART OF RESPONSIBILITY OF ARRIVAL TIME MEASUREMENT

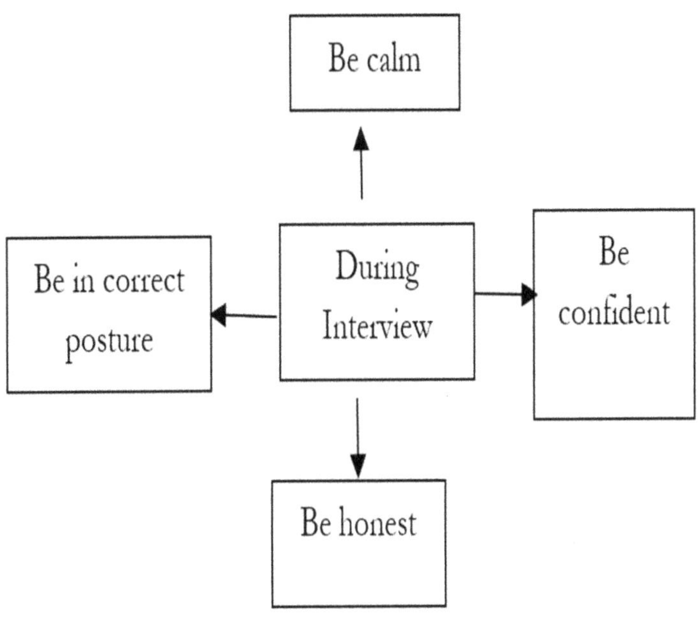

Figure: During Interview

SECTION 3: EXPLANATION OF FLOW CHART ON ARRIVAL ON TIME EXECUTION

The candidate has to follow the four main categories. Be calm, be honest, be in the correct posture, and be confident during the interview. The candidate is to listen to questions properly and reply to the answer accordingly. There should not be misunderstandings of the answers when the candidate is trying to explain the answer in front of the interviewer. The correct postures indicate the candidate is interested in the jobs applied for and has the willingness to work on the job profile. Confidence shows the strength and right ability of the candidate's skill for the requirements imposed by the employer, whether in private or public sector organizations.

PART 3: PROCESS OF DURING THE INTERVIEW

SECTION 1: ABOUT OF PROCESS OF DURING THE INTERVIEW COMMUNICATION

The candidate will first remember to maintain proper eye contact with the interview panel when entering the room. The candidate should wait for any further instructions from the interviewer. The candidate should actively maintain proper attention to body language and eye contact to communicate with the interviewer properly. The candidate will not be selected if their body language is incorrect in front of the interview panel. Hence, the candidate will make sure his or her body language is correct to make proper hand and head movements on the interview panel. The candidate's eye contact should not be forced to see anybody or, particularly, to ignore someone badly. The candidate's behaviour and way of talking were also noticed by the interview panel to select the right candidate.

SECTION 2: FLOWCHART OF PROCESS OF DURING THE INTERVIEW ROUND

The candidate should first Impress with entering with confidence, greet the interviewer (Good morning/afternoon), shake your hands if offered by the interviewer, sit only when invited by the interviewer, Maintain calm posture & eye contact in interview.

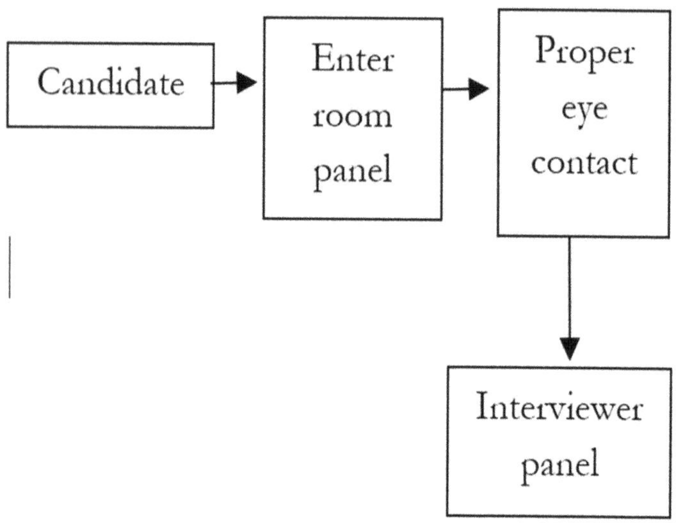

Figure: Interview panel

SECTION 3: EXPLANATION OF FLOW CHART ON INTERVIEW PROCESS DIRECTION

The candidate first enters the room. He or she will communicate with handshaking and proper eye contact and wait for their input. If the panel is telling the candidate to sit, then the candidate will sit on the chair while saying thank you. This discipline impresses the interviewer, and you will be sitting in the chair in a calm and cool manner. While entering the room, their body movement should be proper, and there should not be an extra-ordinary distraction from body movement. The perfection should be displayed in body language, face reorganization, posture, and movement towards the interview panel.

MODULE 5: INTERVIEW ATTENTION DEVELOPING TECHNIQUES

PART 1: ATTENTION OF FIRST IMPRESSIONS

SECTION 1: ABOUT FIRST IMPRESSIONS EXECUTION

The candidate should maintain a smile and body language. It is not about always laughing and smiling. Whenever required by the situation, the candidate shows confidence with a little bit of a smile, and body language should be open to communicate with others properly. There should not be any fear in the interview round. But yes, you do not have to smile so much, which may lead to negative personalities. The interviewer will notice the number of smiles you make in a particular situation. Smiling is not part of the interview, but yes, it shows your level of personality and confidence.

SECTION 2: FLOWCHART OF FIRST IMPRESSIONS DETERMINATION

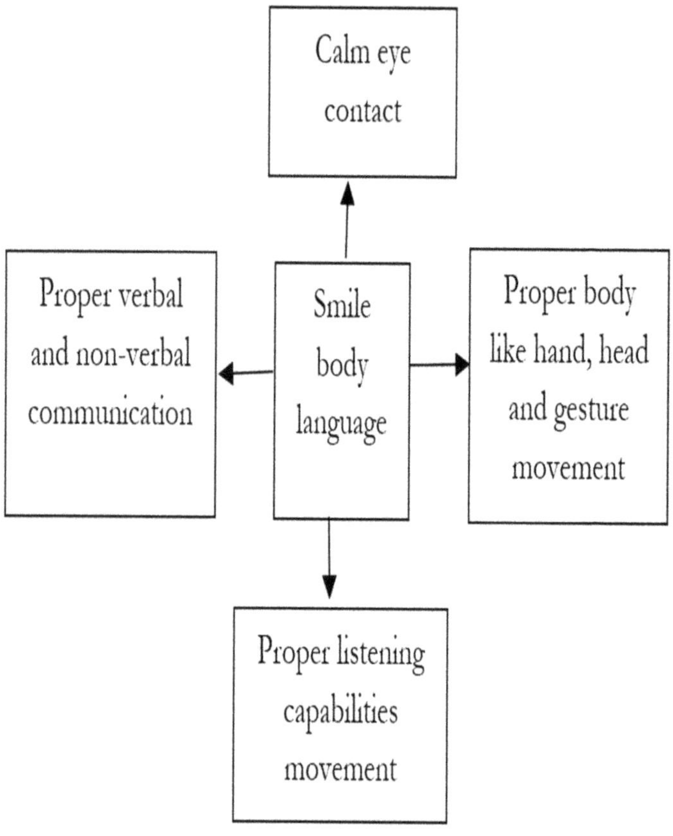

Figure: Interview Impression

SECTION 3: EXPLANATION OF FLOW CHART ON FIRST IMPRESSION TECHNIQUES

The candidate will show interest in the interview panel with the help of proper verbal and non-verbal communication. Proper verbal communication means the way or tone of speaking. Non-verbal means body language, gestures, or movement communication. The candidate should listen properly in the interview, make eye contact, and not be forced to look at someone in uncomfortable situations. The eye contact movement is to be made with the interviewer whenever it is required to explain with non-verbal communication.

PART 2: DEVELOPING OF SMILE BODY LANGUAGE

SECTION 1: DESCRIBE OF SMILE BODY LANGUAGE PROCESS

The candidate must speak clearly, which will be understood by the interviewer. The tone of the speech should not be rude enough to reject the candidature by the interview panel. The way of speaking should be in a confident manner for the candidate to deliver the speech very clearly. If the candidate is not able to speak, then it might be that the interviewer will not be impressed with your profile. Hence, the candidate must speak the sentence clearly and correctly and there should not be any misunderstanding or any pronunciation mistake by the candidate. The interviewer will select candidates whose speaking capabilities are awesome most of the time.

SECTION 2: FLOWCHART OF SMILE BODY LANGUAGE DIRECTION

There are below point makes the effective communications via Smile body language interview communication with strong verbal and non-verbal soft skills.

• Face slightly smiles: The candidate slightly smiled with confidence not over confidence or too much laugh unnecessary cause rejection of the candidature.

• Proper Breathing: The candidate should be in the confidence with proper breathing with inhale and exhale with nose not with mouth.

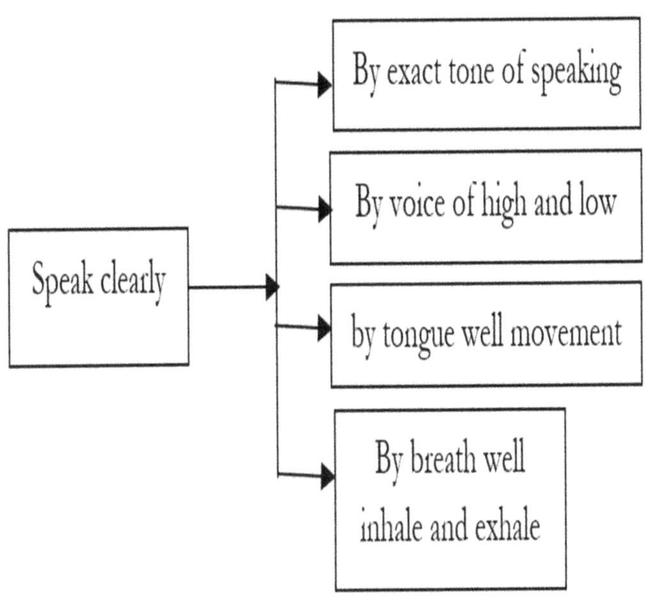

Figure: Interview Language

SECTION 3: EXPLANATION OF FLOW CHART ON BODY LANGUAGE MOVEMENT

The candidate should talk during the interview; his or her sound should not be too loud. It should be normal, which will be comfortable for the interview panel. There are four main categories of well-spoken in front of the interview panel. First, the exact tone of speaking' means that the candidate delivers the speech with confidence, and the voice should be in a balanced mode to speak clearly correctly. The second category, by the voice of high and low speaking, means that the candidate should deliver the word in the fame of sound with a priority of the word to say in a high and low sound manner. If the candidate speaks all words in the same fashion or in the same tone direction, then it will not be impressive for the interviewer to understand the meaning and impact of the sentence. The third category is tongue-well movement, which means that while speaking, your tongue movement should be correct to deliver the right word. The fourth category, breathing well, inhaling and exhaling, means that the breath should be taken properly while speaking. The candidate should inhale, which means taking a breath, and exhale, which means releasing the breath properly. There should be a balance and control of the breath between inhaling and exhaling while delivering the speech in front of the interview panel.

PART 3: TECHNIQUES OF SPEAK CLEARLY

SECTION 1: ABOUT OF SPEAK CLEARLY

The candidate should think first before delivering the answer to the interview panel. The thinking time duration should not be longer, and to be at the right intervals, the speech needs to be delivered. While thinking about any questions, eye contact should be around the panel, and it should not look outside the panel. If the candidate speaks without thinking in front of the interview panel, it might be that the candidate is rejected due to uncertain speaking. The candidate should not deliver the speech without thinking of the correct answers. Thinking is the process of recollecting an idea or knowledge and delivering the correct answers. While thinking, the head and body should not move in a different way. Body language should be proper while thinking in the same direction. While thinking, the candidate should not go outside the room to think or collect ideas.

SECTION 2: FLOWCHART OF SPEAK CLEARLY PROCESS APPROACHES

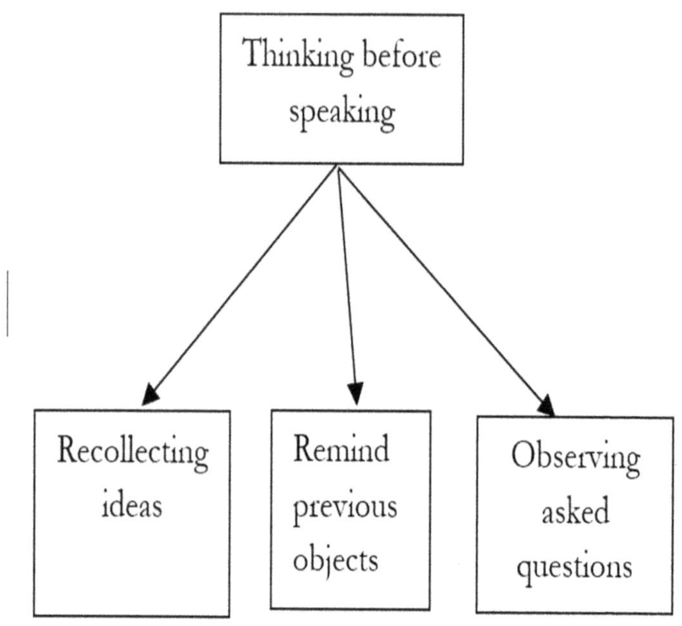

Figure: Interview speaking

SECTION 3: EXPLANATION OF FLOW CHART ON SPEAK CLEARLY TECHNIQUES

The candidate should follow the three categories of thinking before speaking. The first category, recollecting ideas, means that the candidate will remember the already-happening ideas from the past, collect them, and deliver the correct answers to the interview panel. The second category, is reminding previous objects, means that the candidate should look at the previous object or picture to remember the ideas to deliver the answers in front of the interview panel. The third category is observing asked questions, which means the candidate will listen to the interviewer and reply to the answer after analyzing the question asked in the interview panel round.

MODULE 6: INTERVIEW CIRCUMSTANCES BRIEF ANSWERING

PART 1: THINKING BEFORE ANSWERING

SECTION 1: ABOUT BEFORE ANSWERING PROCESS

The candidate should explain the answer in brief. The candidate's good explanation impressed the interviewer. The interviewer will understand that the candidate has in-depth knowledge of the particular topics. The explanation also should not be lengthy. Only the correct answers should be delivered to the interview panel. The explanation should be related to the questions. The answers should not be outside the scope of the questions. The answers should be short with good explanations. According to the type of question asked by the interview panel, the candidate should explain the question accordingly in a precise and calm manner to satisfy the panel.

SECTION 2: FLOWCHART OF BEFORE ANSWERING METHODOLOGIES

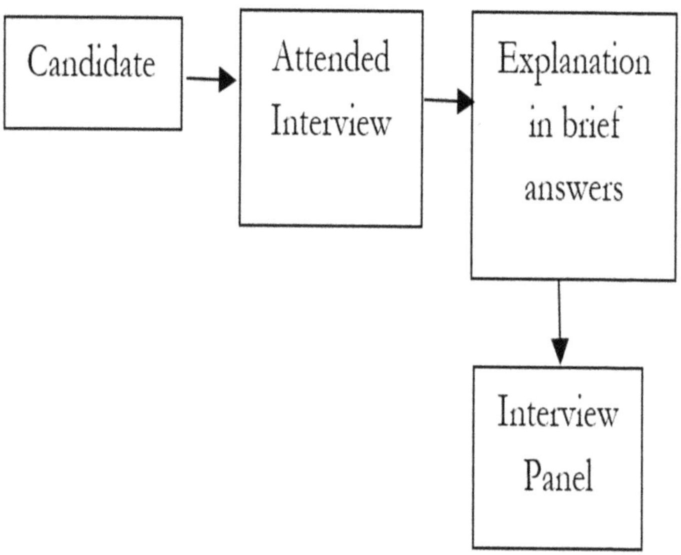

Figure: Interview answers

SECTION 3: EXPLANATION OF FLOW CHART

ON BEFORE ANSWERING APPROACHES

The candidate will start communicating with the interviewer regarding the questions asked by the interviewer. The candidate will recollect the ideas and explain the answer point-wise or with any example that suits the questions. Any real-time example explained by the candidate to the interviewer gives the candidate good chances and credibility to get selected for the interview panel. The candidate will deliver the answer with a real-time example with a pen and paper to show the interviewer any diagram or data flow. Based on the question asked, the candidate should determine whether or not an explanation with an example is required for the requirement. In this case, a short answer with a brief explanation is sufficient for the interview panel.

PART 2: EXPLANATION IN BRIEF ANSWERS
SECTION 1: DESCRIBE OF BRIEF ANSWERS DETERMINATION

The candidate should explain the reason for leaving the company. The interviewer will ask the interviewee what the reason they left their current company or job was.

The candidate should provide the correct information regarding previous employment, experience, and reason for looking for a change of jobs. The candidate should also explain their team-leading experience or support of development activities in past jobs.

SECTION 2: FLOWCHART OF BRIEF ANSWERS EXPLANATIONS PROCESS

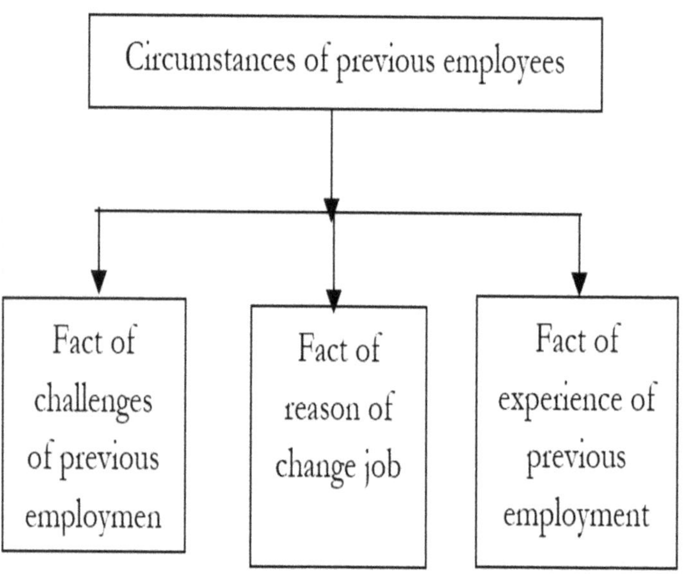

Figure: Interview Explanation

SECTION 3: EXPLANATION OF FLOW CHART ON BRIEF COMMUNICATION

The candidate has three main categories. The first one, Facts of Challenges of Previous Employment, means that the candidate should provide the correct information about previous employment in front of the interview panel. Challenges that the candidate faced in the project or job and how he or she solved the problem. The second category is the fact of the reason for changing jobs, meaning that the candidate should explain the reason for changing jobs. The candidate will answer based on previous employment experience. The candidate may answer the interviewer by saying that he or she is looking for better career growth, better opportunities, or based on his or her willingness to change jobs.

PART 3: CIRCUMSTANCES OF PREVIOUS EMPLOYEES

SECTION 1: ABOUT OF PREVIOUS EMPLOYEES UNDERSTANDING

The candidate must provide correct or truthful information about their experience, project, challenges, achievements, etc. to the interviewer. The candidate should answer with their resume only. It should not be outside of the scope of the resume, as the interviewer is looking at our resume only and observing your experience. The candidate will not keep the wrong information in the resume, which can lead to the candidate being rejected by the interview panel. Hence, the candidate should always mention the correct information. The interviewer will verify the candidate's skills and experience as mentioned in the resume to evaluate the right candidate.

SECTION 2: FLOWCHART OF PREVIOUS EMPLOYEE EXPERIENCES

The candidate should explain with description about previous employment, crisp overview, firm name, your job title and position, employment duration, type of organization. The candidate should explain answer with proper positive reason for leaving organizations like looking for growth, wanting more technical exposure, seeking a stable career, better learning opportunities.

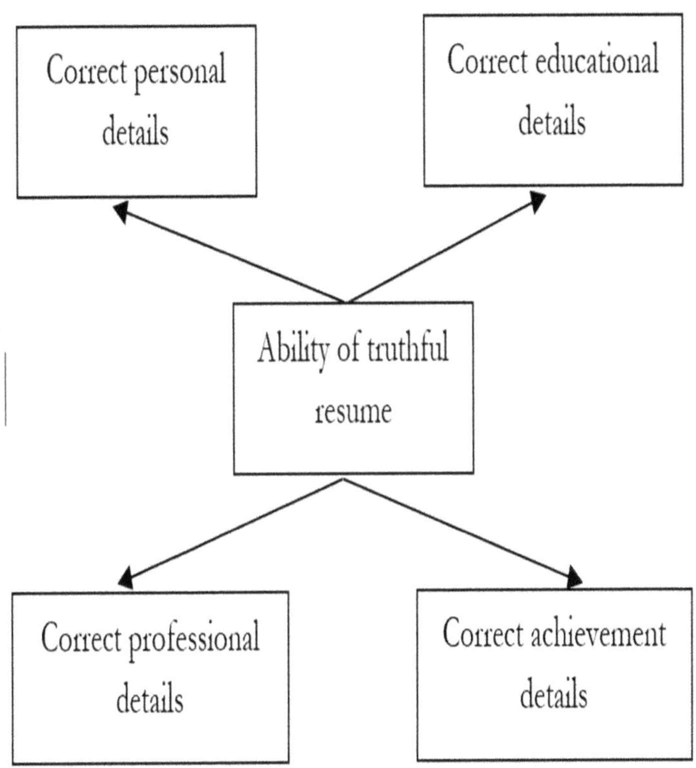

Figure: Interview Experience

SECTION 3: EXPLANATION OF FLOW CHART ON PREVIOUS EMPLOYEE SITUATIONS

The candidate follows the main four categories. The first one is correct personal details, which means that the candidate should mention correct information about the personal details. Personal details mean the communication of address, gender, mobile number, etc. The second category is correct professional details, which means that the candidate should mention in the resume the right experience from past and current employment. Like project details, leading, developing, supporting, etc. The third category is correct achievement details, which means that the candidate gets any award, certificate, etc. to be mentioned in the resume. And the fourth category is correct educational details, which mean that the candidate should mention in the resume a correct degree or diploma certificate and passing year details.

MODULE 7: INTERVIEW ABILITY PROFESSIONAL QUESTIONS

PART 1: ABILITY OF TRUTHFUL RESUMES KNOWING

SECTION 1: ABOUT TRUTHFUL RESUME KNOWING TECHNIQUES

The candidate should think professionally and deliver the answer accordingly to the interviewer. The candidate will speak in front of the interview panel and explain their skills or experiences. The interviewer will see the first personality traits of the candidate, and the candidate should be professional and formal-looking as well to impress the interview panel. The candidate will not think much before delivering the explanation to the interviewer. There should be as quick responses as possible early, but there should not be any wrong statements or misunderstandings of the topics or knowledge sharing with the interviewer.

SECTION 2: FLOWCHART OF TRUTHFUL RESUMES KNOWING PROCESS

The interviewer can ask the question regarding HR of previous company, reporting manager, references provided by you. They also can verify in resume as you mention it as education, skills, personal and professional background, past employment, Roles and responsibilities. Further can be checked as duration, salary code of conduct, no fake gap in education, valid document, valid residential address, identity, etc.

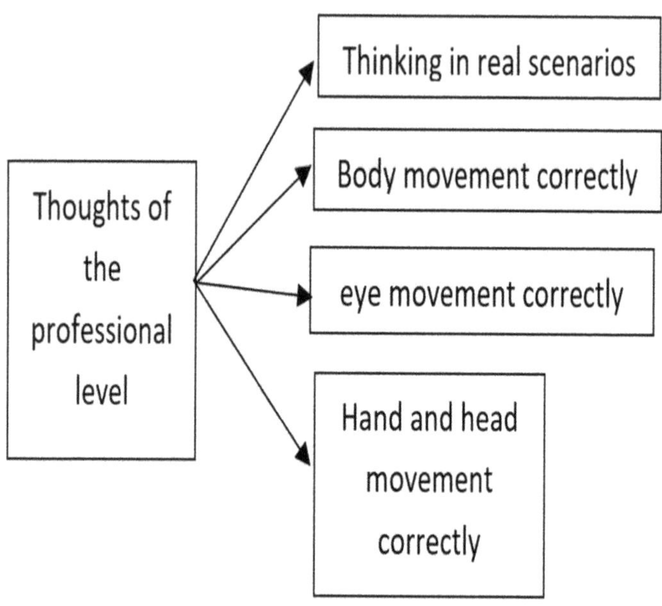

Figure: Interview knowing

SECTION 3: EXPLANATION OF FLOW CHART ON CORRECT RESUME PROCESS

The candidate should follow the main four categories while attending the interview. The first category, thinking about real scenarios, means that the candidate should think about the real scenario of their current or existing employment experience. The second category, 'Body movement correctly' means that the candidate, while entering the room, will stand and move in front of the interview panel, which should show the body movement of the candidate who is interested in applying for the position of employment. The third category, eye movement correctly, means that the candidate should look around at the interviewer and make eye contact whenever required with the interviewer. The fourth category is hand and head movement correctly, which means that the candidate should move the hand and head as per the explanation by the candidate in front of the interview panel. The candidate will do proper hand and head movements, which can impress the interviewer very nicely, giving the candidate a high chance of being selected by the interview panel.

PART 2: THOUGHTS OF PROFESSIONAL LEVEL

SECTION 1: DESCRIBE OF PROFESSIONAL LEVEL THINKING

The candidate will also get common questions from the interviewer, like an introduction, information about their background, and related personal details. The candidate should not feel surprised by the questions asked by the interviewer. The candidate will imagine the question is not related to their skills or experience. It was just to check the mind or ideas of the candidate. Hence, the candidate should not be in a panic. The interview is not about only giving the answer to the interviewer with an explanation of the skills and experiences. It is all about evaluating the candidate perfectly in social, cultural, and other ways. The candidate should prepare for the interview accordingly.

SECTION 2: FLOWCHART OF PROFESSIONAL LEVEL RESEARCH

There are below point makes the effective communications via professional interview communication with strong verbal and non-verbal soft skills.

• Point to point answers: Point to point explanation is more effective and it shows the confidence of the candidate

• Proper real time example: The candidate should explain answer with any kind of the real time example which it could higher chance to get selected in the interview.

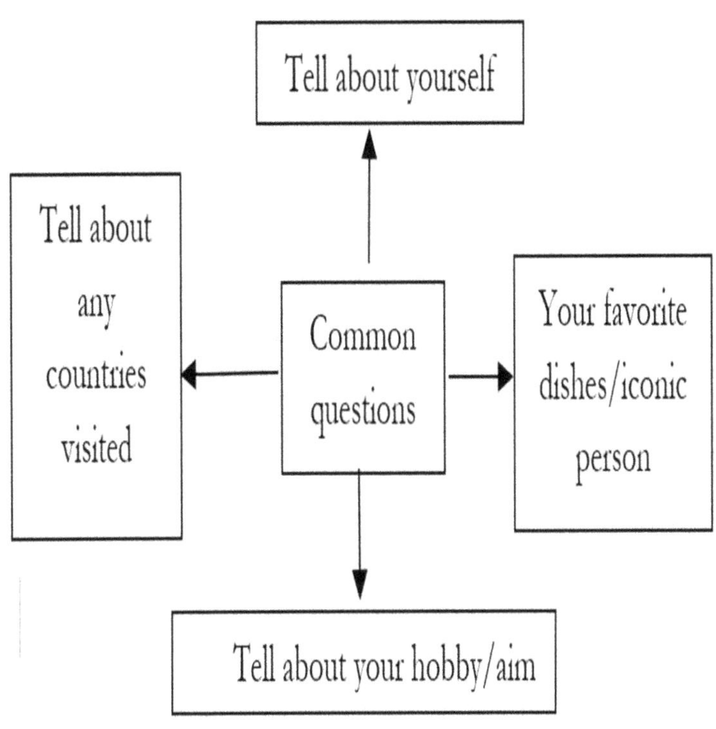

Figure: Interview level

SECTION 3: EXPLANATION OF FLOW CHART ON PROFESSIONAL CHARACTERISTICS

The candidate will get four main categories of questions during the interview. The first category of questions is 'Tell about yourself, which means that the candidate will answer about his personality and personal common details to the interviewer. The second question in the category, Tell about any countries visited, means that the candidate will answer any countries visited with experience and interest in the countries visited. The third category of questions, Tell about your hobby or aim, means that the candidate will answer about their interest in the areas that they like most and their aim or objective in life. The fourth category of the question, your favourite dishes or iconic person, means that the candidate will describe the favourite dishes that he or she most likes and any iconic person that he or she has inspired in life.

PART 3: IMAGINATION OF COMMON QUESTIONS

SECTION 1: ABOUT OF COMMON QUESTIONS DETERMINATION

The interviewer will also expect to hear role-play answers from the candidate. The role-play question means that the question is related to leading the team, what kind of role was played in the previous organization, or having any team-leading experience by the candidate. The interviewer will recognize the development and leading skills in your experience, and preference will be added to the advantages given to the candidate if they have the required skills for leading the team. The candidate should also explain to the interviewer that they have leading experience. The interviewer will ask the candidate if they have any role-play experience in the past or are currently working in the lead role in the organization.

SECTION 2: FLOWCHART OF COMMON QUESTIONS GUIDELINES

The candidate should be focused clear & well structured, honest, focus on skills, match answers with job role, and avoid long or confusing answers. The interviewee should maintain proper positive attitude, show willingness to learn new things, show confidence, not arrogance. The students should avoid saying need higher salary; align with organization direction or instruction by employer.

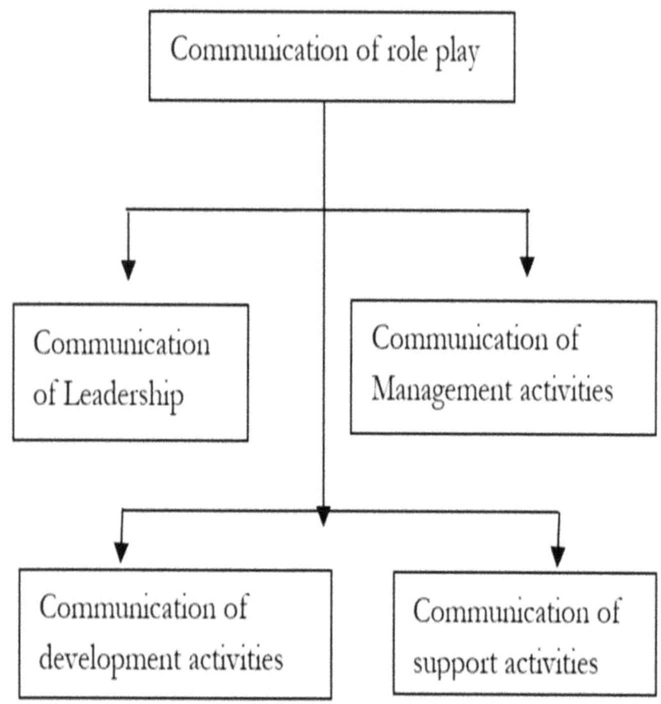

Figure: Interview guidelines

SECTION 3: EXPLANATION OF FLOW CHART ON COMMON QUESTION PROCESS

The candidate will follow the main four categories while facing the interview. The first category of the question is 'Communication of Leadership, which means that the candidate will get the question from the interviewer regarding the leadership skill to know the capabilities of the candidate's leadership. The second category of the question, Communication of Development Activities, means that the candidate will be tested on the development activities with theory or practical approaches by the interviewer. The interview panel will expect the candidate to have strong skills in development activities to meet the needs of the organization. The third category of the question, communication of support activities, means the candidate has experience in providing support, troubleshooting, and handling clients, which is checked by the interview panel. The last fourth category of the question, communication of management activities, means the candidate has management skills like administration, operations, etc. or not, which is checked by the interviewer.

MODULE 8: ROLE PLAY AND PHONE COMMUNICATION QUESTIONS

PART 1: COMMUNICATION OF INDUSTRY SPECIFIC ROLE PLAYS QUESTIONS

SECTION 1: ABOUT ROLE PLAY QUESTIONS

GUIDELINES

The candidate will be evaluated by the interviewer regarding the industry-specific questions. The candidate should have in-depth knowledge of how industry operations work manufacturing, sales, and marketing skills to determine their capabilities in the different areas. If the candidate is applying for a position in an industry company, then the candidate should have knowledge of industry manufacturing processes and industrial infrastructure. The interviewer will ask related industrial questions in a higher-position job like manager or executor to understand the possibilities of working with team members to make an industry successful. The candidate will be selected based on their profile of expertise in the industry and specific experience in current organizations and the interviewer will give preference to the candidate who has the most experience in the field of industry-related.

SECTION 2: FLOWCHART OF ROLE PLAY QUESTIONS DETERMINATION

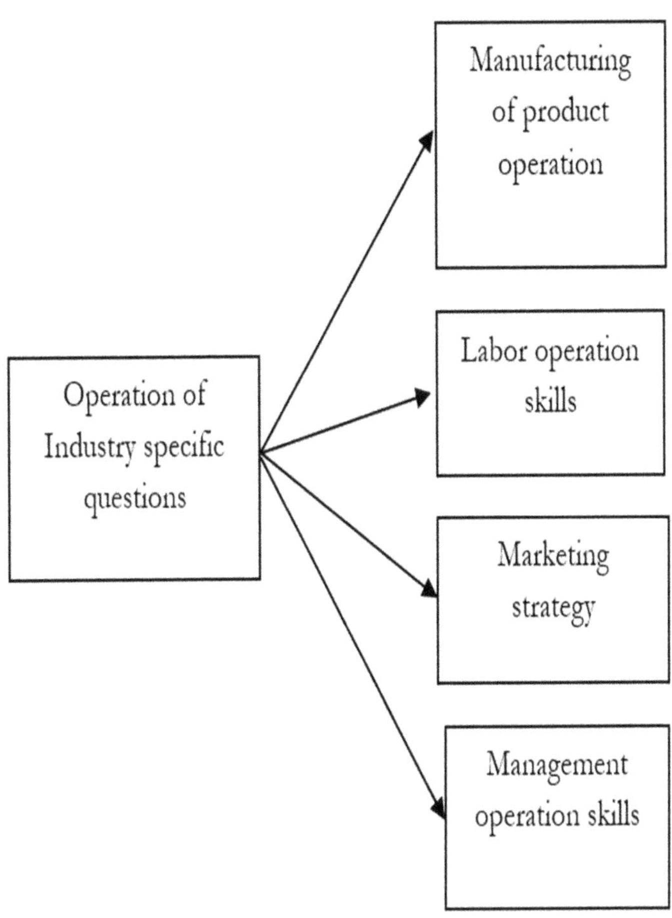

Figure: Interview operation

SECTION 3: EXPLANATION OF FLOW CHART

ON PHONE COMMUNICATION

The candidate will receive the main four categories of questions from the interviewer. The first category of the question is related to manufacturing product operations, meaning that the candidate will be determined by the skills of manufacturing product operations like production and re-manufacturing, the actual cost of the material, and the price estimation of the produced product to be examined by the interview panel. The second category of the question is labour operation skills, which means the candidate will get a question from the interviewer regarding the cost management of the labour operation in the industry. The interviewer will expect to get answers from the candidate related to the labourer's operation, like payment, time, and duration of the contract. The third category of the question is marketing strategy, which means that the candidate will receive questions from the interviewer about marketing strategy like the current market price of the product, the selling price of the product, the manufacturing price of the product, the advertisement price of the product, etc. The interview panel will expect to get the right answer from the candidate regarding knowledge of marketing infrastructure to check the capabilities and skills of the candidate. The interview panel can hire the candidate for the well-known skill of marketing knowledge, and the candidate can get an offer or appointment letter from the employer. And the fourth category of the question, Management Operations Skills, means that the interviewer will expect to get an answer from the candidate regarding the management skills like administration, directorship, execution, and chairperson role skills towards the organization, either in the private or government sector, to be measured to qualify for the interview panel.

PART 2: DEVELOPING PHONE COMMUNICATION INTERVIEW

SECTION 1: ABOUT OF PHONE COMMUNICATION INTERVIEW PROCESS

Today, the candidate will be capable of attending the interview via telephone. Sometimes the organization will ask the candidate to perform a preliminary test abroad. The interviewer will check the skills of the candidate, mostly in the first round of interviews, and will go ahead with phone communication. If the interviewer is satisfied with the candidate, then the candidate will be called for the second round of the interview. It will be either at the technical or management level, as per the requirements expected from the organization.

SECTION 2: FLOWCHART OF PHONE COMMUNICATION INTERVIEW TECHNIQUES

There are below point makes the effective communications via phone interview communication with strong verbal and non-verbal soft skills-

• Check proper phone charging: Make your mobile charged fully and there should not be any battery problem during the interview.

• Check proper Headphone: Check the proper audio sound for both sides of incoming and outgoing audio in mobile.

• Keep other phone away: Do not keep any other phone near during the interview that makes your interview affected due to ringing sound.

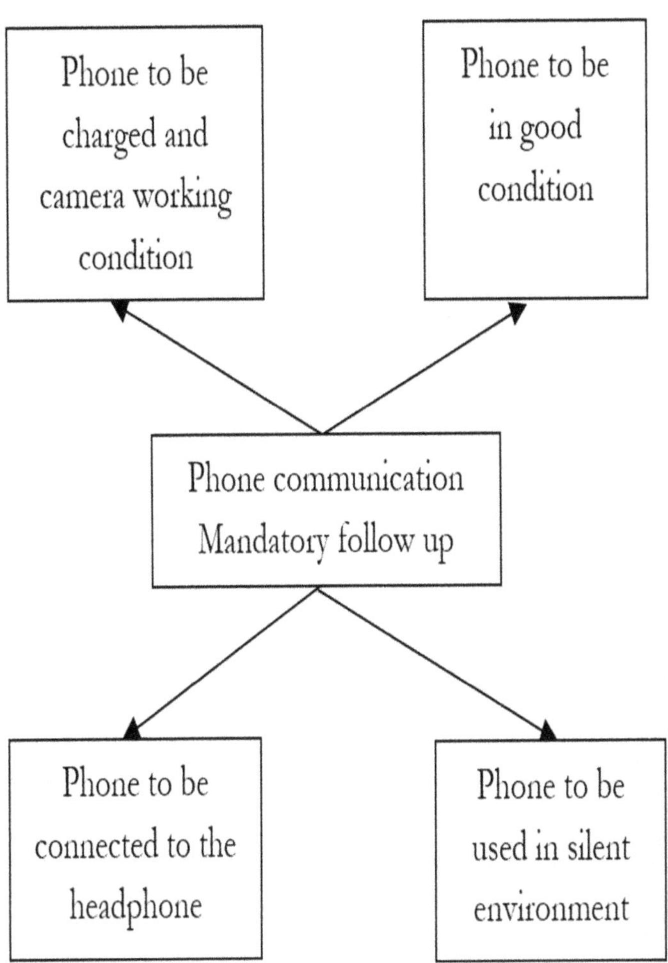

Figure: Interview follow up

SECTION 3: EXPLANATION OF FLOW CHART ON INTERVIEW COMMUNICATION

The candidate will follow four main categories during the interview. The first category of needed is phone to be charged and camera working condition, which means that the candidate will be ready to attend the interview via phone prior to the phone being charged properly, and if the interviewer asks the candidate to be on the camera, then the candidate will be ready to be on the camera and communicate properly. The second category of need is a phone to be connected to the headphone, which means that the candidate will be ready with a headphone connected during an interview phone call. There should not be disconnected headphones during the interview call. The third category of need is a phone to be used in a silent environment to attend the interview call, which means that the candidate will be available in a silent place to listen properly to the interviewer. There should not be any noise around the interview call. The last fourth category of needed is the phone to be in good condition, which means that the candidate will keep the phone in good condition, like there should not be any mobile audio problems, very low network detection, or a phone hanging condition. The interviewer will check the manner in which the candidate handled the interview. If the interviewer thinks that the candidate maintained a good environment with phone communication, it is a good sign that the candidate can clear the first round of the interview successfully.

MODULE 9: VIDEO CONFERENCE AND VOICE COMMUNICATION

PART 1: VIDEO CONFERENCE VIA LAPTOP COMMUNICATION

SECTION 1: ABOUT LAPTOP VIDEO CONFERENCE OVERVIEWS

The candidate will face the interview via laptop video conference with the interview panel. The interviewer will expect a well-maintained laptop without any issues with audio, video, or sharing of the document and a chat box enabled in the video conference interview call. The candidate will be connecting the headphones for better sound transfer during communication with the interview panel. The candidate will get an invitation from the employer or organization for the video conference. The candidate should accept the meeting to show interest in the position for which he or she applied. The candidate should attend the interview 5 to 10 minutes early to make a note to prepare to attend the interview.

SECTION 2: FLOWCHART OF LAPTOP INTERVIEW COMMUNICATION

There are below points makes the effective communications via laptop interview communication with strong verbal and non-verbal soft skills-

• Good internet: A stable connection makes a perfect choice of good communication and should be closed unnecessary program makes reduce the speed of the internet.

• Test software application: Check your meeting application is installed properly there should not be any upgrading required during the interview.

• Test hardware device: Check your laptop's camera and microphone and audio are working fine.

• Adjust your web camera: Make your body in centre and slightly straight face toward camera and looking at camera point.

Interview Cracking in First Attempt

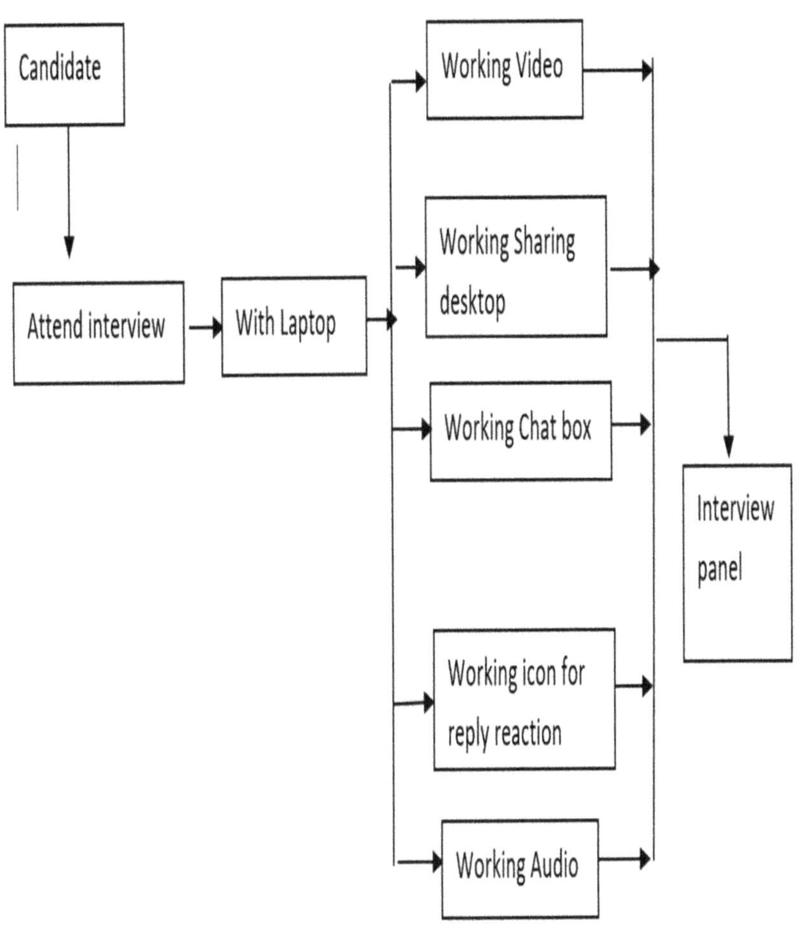

Figure: Interview Laptop communication

SECTION 3: EXPLANATION OF FLOW CHART ON LAPTOP VIDEO CONFERENCE

The candidate will first attend the interview with a laptop. The candidate will verify everything is working fine, like video, sharing desktop, chat box, the icon for reply reaction, and audio. The candidate should be ready to connect to the headphones and will be waiting for the interviewer to join the meeting. The laptop should not be hung out or restarted automatically. There should not be any technical issue with the laptop to disturb the interview call.

PART 2: VOICE TONE TECHNIQUES

SECTION 1: DESCRIBE OF VOICE TONE METHODOLOGIES

The candidate will calmly maintain the tone of voice. There should not be a high and rude voice during the interview. The candidate should reply to the question in a very polite manner to impress the interviewer. The candidate should speak properly and correctly, and the answer or word should not be repeated again and again.

There should not be speed in delivering the answer. Wherever required, the pause or slowness of the point or sentence is to be followed to make it very clear in front of the interview panel.

SECTION 2: FLOWCHART OF VOICE TONES EXPERIENCE PROCESS

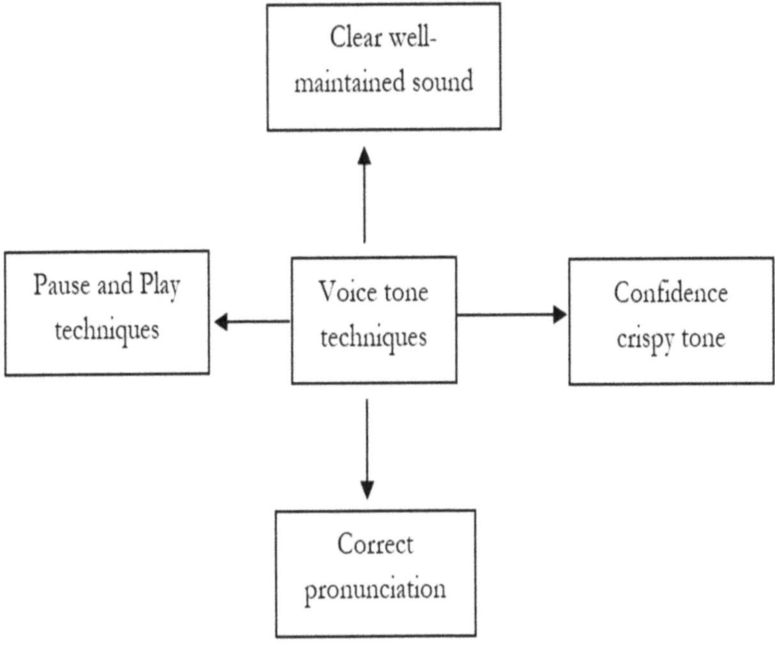

Figure: Interview tone

SECTION 3: EXPLANATION OF FLOW CHART ON VOICE TONES TECHNIQUES

The candidate will follow the voice tone technique with four major categories while speaking in front of the interviewer. The first category is clear, well-maintained sound, which means that the candidate should speak with correct grammar in order to explain any question asked by the interview panel. If the sentence is pronounced wrong, then the interviewer may not understand what you are saying as an answer. The second category, Pause and Play Techniques, means that the candidate should speak with a proper pause if the particular sentence is finished with a dot mark. And play means that from pause to the dot mark at the end of the sentence, and after the dot mark, it will start speaking the sentence until any comma or dot is mentioned in the sentence. The third category, correct pronunciation, means that the candidate should speak with the correct pronunciation. If the pronunciation is incorrect, then the meaning will be totally changed. Example: Sit and Sheet If you see that the pronunciation is the same but a little bit of pause speed is observed while speaking a sit-and-sheet, the pronunciation is to be practiced by the candidate to make the statement understandable to the interview panel. The last category is 'confidence. Crispy Tone, meaning that the candidate should speak confidently and the tone should be crispy, meaning more actively speaking and not kind of dull speaking in front of the interview panel.

MODULE 10: RESUME PREPARATION GUIDELINES AND CONVERSATION

PART 1: ABOUT RESUME PREPARATION GUIDELINES

SECTION 1: ABOUT RESUME PREPARATION PROCESS

The candidate will follow up on the guidelines for resume preparation. A resume is an important part of any interview process. The interview involves your personal and professional details, which are reviewed by the interviewer or employer. The resume is a first impression in which the candidate is screened for the first level of the employment requirements of any organization.

SECTION 2: RESUME PREPARATION STEPS OF TECHNIQUE

There are the following guidelines to be followed while preparing the resume:

1. Mention the name at the top of the page, in the middle centre.

2. Keep any certifications on top of the page on the left side.

3. Mention the address at the top of the page.

4. Mention the mobile number left at the top of the page.

5. Mention the email address on the top right side of the page.

6. After you put how many years of experience with technology or specific work

7. Mention expert details.

8. Mention your career objective.

9. Mention employment at your previous and current jobs.

10. Mention technical tools, operating systems, and databases.

11. Mention education qualification details.

12. Mention any training and certification details.

13. Mention project or work details from previous or current employment.

14. Mention personal details.

SECTION 3: FLOWCHART OF RESUME PREPARATION DETERMINATION

The candidate must mention in resume like Header Name, Phone, Email, LinkedIn or any certified logo, professional summary, skills, experience, projects, education, certifications, achievements, prizes. Interviewers instantly judge like font, spacing, alignment, bullet points, grammar, etc. In resume better to recommend formatting font: Calibri, Arial, and font size 10–12

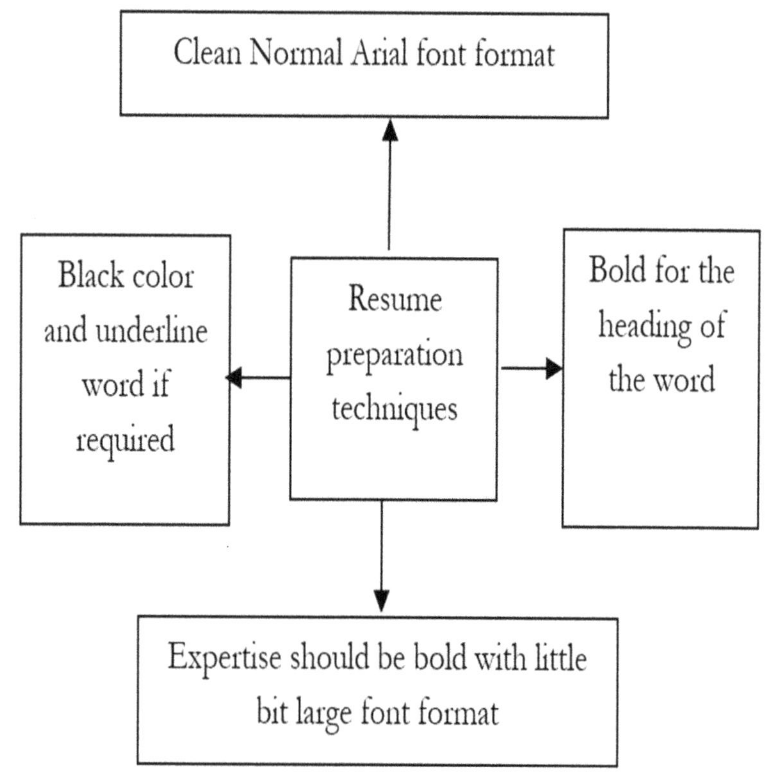

Figure: Resume preparation

SECTION 4: EXPLANATION OF FLOW CHART ON RESUME CREATION

The resume preparation technique has four major categories needed for the perfect resume. The first category is 'Clean Arial font format, which means that the font to be selected is Normal. It is most preferable to select Arial and a font size of 12 for a resume. The second category of the technique is black color and underlining words if required, meaning that the font color to be selected is black. Preferably not to mention any dark color. Text to be underlined wherever required in the resume, which too is highlighted in the resume. The third category of the technique is expertise should be bold with a little bit of a large font format, which means that work experience should be bold with a little bit of a large font format to be highlighted in the resume. The interview will focus most of the time on the bold one, which is a resume that shows the expertise of the work and technology. The fourth category technique is bold for the heading of the word, which means that the heading of the line is bold to understand the details of the Heading. Example names, skills, project names, etc.

PART 2: REAL TIME CONVERSATION
SECTION 1: DESCRIPTION ON REAL TIME CONVERSATION

The candidate should be fit physically and mentally to attend the interview. The physical is called external personality, which impressed the interviewer. The first impression of the fitness of the candidate will be noticed during the interview by the interviewer. The interviewer will look into whether the candidate also has a healthy body. As we say, a healthy body has a healthy mind. The mental power of skills like behaviour, stress, a positive mind, and expertise in skills are to be observed by the employer or interviewer.

SECTION 2: FLOWCHART OF REAL TIME COMMUNICATION TECHNIQUES

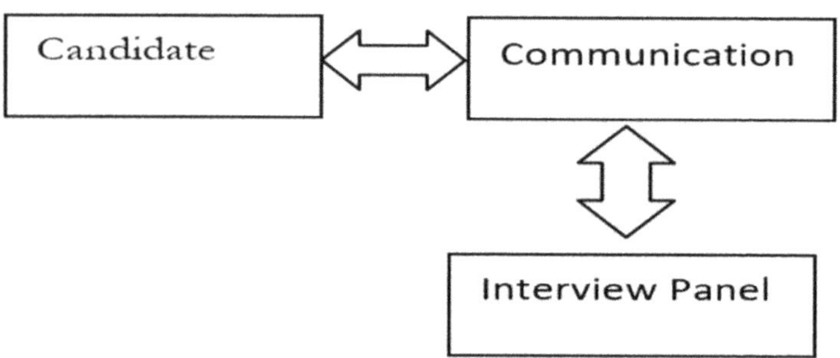

Figure: Interview flow

SECTION 3: EXPLANATION OF FLOW CHART ON REAL TIME PROCESS APPROACHES

The candidate will communicate properly with the interview panel to get selected for the interview round. And the interviewer will communicate with the candidate to evaluate the candidate in the interview discussion. There will be two-way communication with each other to find out which candidate is eligible for the job selected by the interviewer. All communication will be conducted physically at the office or via telephone or video conference, whichever is required, to select the right candidate by the interviewer.

SECTION 4: REAL TIME CONVERSATION DISCUSSION & FREQUENTLY ASKED QUESTIONS (FAQ): QUESTIONS WITH DESCRIPTIVE ANSWERS

There are the following real-time conversations between the candidate and the interviewer:

Question: 1. Interview panel: Good morning, Name of the candidate

Answer: Candidate: Good morning, Name of the interviewer

Question: 2. Interview panel: Tell me about yourself, your experience, and your role responsibilities.

Answer: Candidate: It is a pleasure to introduce myself here. My total year of experience is 'number of total experience'. I am working as 'Position Name in Organization Name." I have expertise in technology or work in expert detail. My educational qualification is 'degree name'. I have completed the certification 'details of the certification done'. I am currently staying in 'Place Name." My native place is 'home town name'. My role in the current organization is to lead the team and work on development, support, and guiding the junior team members. I have done the 'number of the project'. I have domain knowledge in e-commerce, marketing, telecom, healthcare, banking, etc. That's all about myself.

Question: 3. Interview panel: Well, I will start with technical skills and management skills questions.

Answer: Candidate: Sure

Question: 4. Interview Panel: Describe your current project.

Answer: Candidate: My current project is 'XYZ. I have used technical skills like technology name, and this project is based on the banking domain, and the team size is 10. This project has this module, which is used to maintain the record of the fixed deposits of the customers. The customer will fill in all the details of the fixed deposit, like tenure, amount, and renewal of the fixed deposit. We have done the coding, design, development, and support for the project. Or the candidate will explain what work or experience you have had.

Question: 5. Interview panel: Good. Tell me about the challenges you face in your work or project.

Answer: Candidate: My challenge was in the project, as it was complex and I was not able to fix one of the issues. My team leader helped and inspired me to do the fix. I went through the document, understood the business flow of the project, and practiced myself to improve my coding or work skills.

Question: 6. Interview panel: Okay, what is the greatest achievement you have made in your organization?

Answer: Candidate: I was the best performer in my team for leading the project and team members.

Question: 7. Interview panel: Where do you see yourself after 5 years?

Answer: Candidate: I will see myself in 5 years as a Technical Manager or architect, and I will be updating and upgrading my skills towards the growth of the organization.

Question: 8. Interview panel: What are your weaknesses and strengths?

Answer: Candidate: My weakness is working too hard, and my strength is upgrading and learning myself technically quickly and being passionate about working with a team to resolve the issue of the project for the success of the organization.

Question: 9. Interview Panel: Why will they hire you?

Answer: Candidate: I am technically strong, which helps the success of the organization towards project growth, support, and development.

Question: 10. Interview panel: Ok, will you work overtime if required urgently to complete some work?

Answer: Candidate: Yes, definitely. I am passionate about working hard to complete the task if it requires urgent overtime.

Question: 11. Interview panel: Fine. Why do you leave a current organization?

Answer: Candidate: Because I worked hard in my previous organization and participated in the growth and success of the company. I wanted to add new challenges to the growth and development of the next company and use my upgraded skills to ensure its success.

Question: 12. Interview panel: Why do you want to work for this organization?

Answer: Candidate: I went through the understanding of the company details, and I am impressed with this company's development research, technology, and support, which makes me grow myself, and I was able to contribute my technical skills to the success of this organization.

Question: 13. Interview panel: Do you have experience leading team members?

Answer: Candidate: Tell me no if you do not have it or have not handled it in a previous company, and you can say if I am getting a new role of leading opportunity, I can make myself upgrade my leading skills for a team playing for the requirements of the organization. Tell yes if you have worked before leading the team.

I am very well equipped to handle the team member, and I was handling agile methodologies or daily status meetings to check the team member's status and was reporting to the project manager.

Question: 14. Interview panel: Will you agree to relocate the job if required?

Answer: Candidate: Yes, I am willing to relocate myself whenever required for the success and growth of the organization.

Question: 15. Interview panel: What are your salary expectations for your current job?

Answer: Candidate: I will be looking forward to more work on enhancing technologies for the success of the organization. My salary expectation is based on my current company's salary hike of 30%. I will be engaged in the work assignment and exploring my experience in this organization, as I have strong skills in the development and support of the application.

Question: 16. Interview panel: How do you handle your job and personal life successfully?

Answer: Candidate: The candidate should explain the balance between work and personal life. The candidate must show an interest in the working environment of the company and simultaneously show an interest in personal life. The critical and high-priority assignment is definitely to work around the success of the organization to adjust the family accordingly to manage the personal life.

Question: 17. Interview panel: Do you have any questions? You want to ask?

Answer: Candidate: This is the most frequently asked question from the interviewer at the end of the interview. This is a good chance for the candidate to explore his or her skills or knowledge and get ideas or views from the interviewer. May I know which domain belongs to the current project for this requirement? Do we have any transport facilities with this company to travel to the office? You will not be asking more questions, but yes, at least one question should be asked by the candidate to show interest in the current organizations.

MODULE 11: QUESTIONS WITH DESCRIPTIVE ANSWERS AND PRACTICES

Question: 1. what is the objective of this course?

Description- To improve the communication between interviewer and interviewee and the interviewee will learn to crack the interview with personal and professional experience. It does not only enhance the behavior of the person. It improves the complete personality of the candidate. An interview is a formal conversation between an interviewer and interviewee where the former seeks answers from the latter, which checks their capability in joining the desired post. When broken down into two separate terms, interviews are 'inter' and 'view,' meaning exchanging ideas each other. It will not only improve the management skill. It also improves the candidate's overall personal and professional skills. It does not only improve functional and logical behavior. It improves the personal and professional skills

Question: 2. who gets benefited with this course?

Description- For all students and professionals. This course is mainly designed for all students and professionals. This course provides an understanding of a student or professional's strengths and weaknesses. As you get to know the best techniques to follow up during the interview process, it may help you determine how they can best leverage their abilities in the private or public sector organization.

Question: 3. what is the need of interview?

Description- An interview is the process of evaluating the skills and personalities of the candidate. An interview is the process of evaluating the skills and personalities of the candidate. The employer will select the right candidate who belongs to fit the requirement of the company.

Question: 4. what is the best way of cracking the interview?

Description- Be precise and focused. The candidate is to be focused on the skills demanded by the employer and to be precise with revising and practice the job description of the company.

Question: 5. How to improve the communication skills?

Description- Listen and talk professionally. Communication can be improved by first listening capability and then start talking.

Question: 6. what is an interview and how it be defined?

Description- An interview is a formal conversation between an interviewer and interviewee. An interview is a formal conversation between an interviewer and interviewee. An interview is a process of handling the team member in the organization to support the members of the company

Question: 7. What Interviewer will check and test the candidate?

Description- The interviewer will be looking for a candidate who has good skills matches with company requirement. The interviewer will be looking for a candidate who has good skills that match with company's requirements. The interview is conducted based on the requirements needed in the organization matches with the right candidate skills.

Question: 8. who is called as Interviewer?

Description- The interviewer is called also an employer, and organization. The interview, who takes the interview and select the right candidate or interviewee.

Question: 9. who is called interviewee?

Description- The interviewee who attend the interview same as the candidate. The interviewer is the same as a candidate who attends the interview for the job. The interviewer is the same as a candidate who attends the interview for the job

Question: 10. When the Interview started around?

Description- Around 1921. The conduct of the Interview started around 1921.

Question: 11. When a candidate can be rejected?

Description- The candidate can be rejected for the inappropriate behavior

Question: 12. What is the meaning of career?

Description- Career is the variety of experiences that you have undertaken throughout your life. It is the combination of your life experience, learning, and all work experience. These days, you are responsible for your career and you have to continuously reflect on where you are, where you want to be and how you will prepare for further career opportunities

Question: 13. What is the meaning of self-evaluation?

Description- Self-evaluation is the process of systematically observing, analyzing and improving one's own actions or result. Self-evaluation is the process of systematically observing, analyzing and improving one's own actions or result

Question: 14. What is pre planned interview approaches?

Description- Keep mobile in silent mode and revised the highlighted points before attending the interview. Always mobile should be in silent or switched off mode to concentrate mind prepared and ready to face the interview

Question: 15. What is the best practice for self-evaluation?

Description- Do your research and record yourself to replay the video or audio. Do yourself a favor and keep track of your projects throughout the year. Self-evaluation is the process of systematically observing, analyzing and improving one's own actions or results. Self-evaluations give you the chance to showcase yourself to the manager and the company as a valuable asset.

Question: 16. What are the main categories of self-evaluation?

Description- Observation, analyzing, comparison and abilities. Self-assessment provides students with an opportunity to self-evaluate, or make judgments about their learning process and products of learning. Observation, analyzing, comparison and abilities are the main categories to perform well in interview and the company you believe are important and any professional beliefs you strive to uphold. His type of 'selfing' behavior has clear overlap with the cognitive process category.

Question: 17. Who applied for the job vacancy?

Description- Interviewee. The Interviewer who is taking the interview. The Employer who arrange the interview.

A company is described as a voluntary association of persons who have come together for carrying on business and sharing the profits. a person who answers questions in an interview about a product or service

Question: 18. Doctors will apply most of the time in the same organizational profile. Select the best answer

Description- Hospital. Doctors will apply most of the time in same organization profile. The doctor will apply most of the time in the Hospital. The doctor will apply rarely in Railways if the Railways required the Doctors. The doctor will rarely apply in the school department if the requirement is announced by the private or government sectors.

Question: 19. What kind of clothes candidate can wear in an interview?

Description- Formal. A causal dress is not preferable. Colourful dress is not suitable in interview. Formal dress to be preferred in the interview. A dark colour dress is not preferable

Question: 20. What is mock interview?

Description- A mock interview is a process of practicing the existing set of already asked questions and practicing for the answers. Mock interviews are like the study of a practical approach to build your skills and ability to perform best in interviews.

Question: 21. What are research methodologies in terms of Interviews?

Description- An interview is a analytical research method that depend on asking questions and collecting the refined and truthful data. The candidate research on the truthful data to develop analytical skills.

Question: 22. When candidate should be arrived to attend the interview?

Description- At least 10 to 15 minutes earlier. The candidate should arrive at the interview venue on time 10 to 15 minutes earlier to prepare the mindset to attend the interview. The arrival time should not cross the time of the scheduled interview.

Question: 23. When candidate can be rejected by the interview panel?

Description- After interview time elapsed. The candidate can be rejected for not attending an interview on time.

Question: 24. What discipline candidate should maintain during the interview?

Description- Listen properly and reply the answer accordingly. The candidate to maintain calm and cool to understand and listen the question properly and reply the answer accordingly.

Question: 25. How the candidate can improve confident?

Description- Monitor Your Progress and talk fearless. Monitor Your Progress and talk fearless. The best way to improve the goals either big or small to break them into smaller parts of the goal. If the candidate fails then try again and again and achieve success fearless.

Question: 26. When a candidate enters the interview panel room then what should he or she does?

Description- Stand with good posture and saying Good Morning. Stand with good posture. The candidate should greet the interviewers by saying Good Morning.

Question: 27. What is the first impression of the interviewee?

Description- Face and dress. The first impression is the process of when the interviewer sees the interviewee first time and observed his or her personality.

Question: 28. What is smile body language?

Description- A sincere smile. The interviewee will smile only in the amount of the situation of the condition required. It is a about body posture.

Question: 29. What is verbal communication?

Description- Verbal communication means the process of exchanging ideas and views with two or more persons.

Question: 30. What is nonverbal communication?

Description- Nonverbal communication means that the without voice communication

Question: 31. How to speak with clear and good tone voice in interview?

Description: A good tone of voice is a higher chance of selection in the interview and added advantage for the employer.

Question: 32. What candidate can think before attending the interview?

Description- The candidate should keep their mobile off to not make any disturbance before attending the interview.

Question: 33. What interviewer can expect to hear from the candidate with previous experience?

Description- Interviewers looks the right information with respect of the candidate.

Question: 34. How Interviewer can select the best resume of the candidate?

Description- Interviewers select the best resume to evaluate the candidature.

Question: 35. How resume can be rejected by an employer?

Description- Candidates put too much personal information in a resume like Marital Status, Height, Weight, etc. This information in your resume can be termed as negatively and rejected by interviewer.

Question: 36. Who is the recruiter or Employer?

Description- A recruiter searches qualified candidates for a job and works with and Employer who organizes the interview process to select the right candidate or interviewee.

Question: 37. What is the meaning of a truthful resume?

Description- A truthful resume indicates that the fact of the right information of the candidate.

Question: 38. What is professional-level thinking?

Description- The candidate should not be limited to except the question of only personal experience by the interviewer. It could be related to environment science and historical philosophy.

Question: 39. What is the common question asked by the interviewer? Select best choice.

Description: The Interviewer will ask the question related to social and cultural activities and knowledge of the candidate. The question can be like tell me about your favorite dishes and iconic persons.

Question: 40. What is the meaning of leadership?

Description-Leadership means that for encouraging people or groups of people.

Question: 41. What are management activities?

Description- Management activity is related to the Administrative organization.

Question: 42. What is an industry specific role play question?

Description- Industry-specific questions are related to the environment of production, manufacturing, distribution, and marketing skills

Question: 43. What is the role of phone communication in the interview?

Description- The interviewer will call to the interviewee by the Phone or Mobile to evaluate the candidate skill or knowledge. The interviewer most of the time will call to the interviewee for first round of the interview to observe the candidate.

Question: 44. In which condition phone should be maintained at the time of the telephonic interview?

Description-The candidate must charge the mobile fully before attending the telephonic call to avoid the degradation of the continuous call cut chances. The candidate should connect to headphone to communicate properly without any distraction of the environment.

Question: 45. What is a telephonic interview? Select best answer.

Description- Telephonic interviews are established by the organization to select the right candidate based on the private or government organization requirement. A phone interview is a pre-planned scheduled time to conduct a interview by interviewer.

Question: 46. What is a video interview?

Description- It saves time to interviewee go to any interview location. It is not directly a physical face-to-face interview but it is a digital video face-to-face interview.

Question: 47. What is a video conference?

Description- Video conference is the process of interacting with people or groups of people face-to-face via digital media.

Question: 48. How to improve better voice tone in the interview?

Description- The speaking should not be fast. The candidate has to stop the sentence and be paused and start the new sentence with confidently. There should not be stress while delivering the speaking with interviewer.

Question: 49. What are the resume preparation techniques?

Description- The candidate should prepare a resume with clean concise font and avoid mentioning wrongful information.

Question: 50. What should be the size of the resume?

Description- Resume size should be A4 standard letter size (8.5" x 11") paper.

Question: 51. What is the meaning of a resume?

Description- The interviewer will evaluate the candidate resume first and ask most of the question related to the resume. Resume indicates that the candidate identification of the job type applicable with respected organization requirement.

Question: 52. How do you physically prepare for attending an interview?

Description- Yoga is the best way to reduce stress and stretch your muscles and exercise makes your energetics

Question: 53. How do you mentally prepare for attending an interview?

Description- The candidate should develop the skill of reading and writing practice exercise

Question: 54. How does the candidate interact with the interviewer?

Description- The candidate must greet with a handshake.

Question: 55. What is the difference s between resume and bio data?

Description - It is details about the skills, personal details, experience, and educational information. Biodata summarizes more by providing details of your experience

Question: 56. What is the meaning of CV?

Description - CV stands that Curriculum Vita

MODULE 12: PRACTICE TEST AND ASSIGNMENT

Question1: Write the steps to make a perfect resume. (At least 300 hundred words)

Question2: Write the precaution of before attending the interview (At least 400 hundred words)

Question3: If someone gets unselected in first round of the interview. How candidate should crack the interview in second round. What are the pre-planned to make it interview successfully.

Question4: If the interviewer is asking questions to the candidate about different skills which is not matched to the candidate profile. What candidate should tell to the interviewer?

Question5: If the candidate is waiting for the interview very long time in the interview place. What the approached the candidate should take it for interview done.

MODULE 13: RECAP/SUMMARIZATION

There are the following guidelines, tips, and tricks for the preparation of a resume, as well as precautions and reasons for rejecting the resume by the interviewer in the interview screening.

Preparation of a resume: pre-planning

1. We must first mention your name at the top of the page.
2. We must mention the name, email address, and mobile number.
3. We have to add the logo of any certification you have.
4. We should add a local address on the right side of the resume.
5. We should make a border for the executive summary, and the colour may be grey.
6. We have to mention how much experience you have with your technology and skills.

7. We need to mention your strengths and executive summary.
8. We need to mention your domain experience.
9. We must mention some of your expert technical experience.
10. We must mention if you travelled aboard.
11. We must mention if you have a US visa.
12. We must add a DD career objective header with a grey colour.
13. We should mention your career aim and objective.
14. We have to add employment details from the starting jobs you worked in the organization below the employment profile section; add all company names where you worked and include your experiences.
15. We must add the educational, technical, certification, and training details if the candidate has any.
16. Add the project details, your responsibility for the project, the size of the team, and the period of the project.

Precautions for Resume:-Safeguard

1. We should not use big or large fonts and colours in your resume. We must make simple and readable text formats up to 12 or 14, and font styles prefer to be Arial. We should not make more than font size 14 and font style times in roman with bold letter font style. We should create your heading with more than 13 sizes below 16 of the font text.
2. We must not put any picture, like a phone number, email, or some organizational picture, in the resume.
3. We should not mention your family details in your resume. If the interviewer is asking for family details, then we should describe your family details orally to the interviewer.
4. We should not mention the salary details in the resume, and probably they will be asked in HR or the final round only.
5. We should not scratch your text until it is required. Probably leave it on your resume.
6. Use italic fonts until required in the resume. It requires some of the time, like an alternate email if it is applicable.

7. We do not describe your project much, and there are more than 15 lines in the resume.
8. We should not take a printout of the resume on both sides of the page. It should be A4, or letter size, which is the standard size of a resume.
9. We should not mention the picnic or trip details in our resume.
10. We do not fold your resume and keep your resume in proper

Cover Letter: Upload your resume to naukri.com along with your cover letter. The cover letter describes mainly your professional salary details and the type of employment…….

Reference link-

https://notionpress.com/read/interview-cracking-in-first-attempt

https://www.udemy.com/course/interview-cracking-in-first-attempt

Interview Kit free download link-

https://sites.google.com/view/eml-groups/seminar/interview-kit

www.ingramcontent.com/pod-product-compliance
Lightning Source LLC
Chambersburg PA
CBHW041333120726

48005CB00014B/2230